AF577053

Super Prayerables

To Add a Glow to your Life

Other books by Irene Burk Harrell

PRAYERABLES: MEDITATIONS OF A HOMEMAKER

GOOD MARRIAGES GROW: A BOOK FOR WIVES

GOD VENTURES:
TRUE ACCOUNTS OF GOD IN THE LIVES OF MEN

LO, I AM WITH YOU: PRAYERSTEPS TO FAITH
(charisma edition entitled MIRACLES THROUGH PRAYER)

ORDINARY DAYS WITH AN EXTRAORDINARY GOD:
PRAYERABLES II

THE OPPOSITE SEX (with Allen Harrell)

MUDDY SNEAKERS AND OTHER FAMILY HASSLES

SECURITY BLANKETS—FAMILY SIZE

THE WINDOWS OF HEAVEN: PRAYERABLES III

MULTIPLIED BY LOVE

BLACK TRACKS, by Floyd Miles, as told to Irene Burk Harrell

GOD'S LIVING ROOM, by Herbert Walker, with Irene Burk Harrell

HOW TO LIVE LIKE A KING'S KID, by Harold Hill,
as told to Irene Burk Harrell

HOW TO BE HAPPY IN NO MAN'S LAND, by Iverna Tompkins,
edited by Irene Burk Harrell

FROM GOO TO YOU BY WAY OF THE ZOO?
by Harold Hill, as told to Irene Burk Harrell

SOMETHING FOR NOTHING, by Sid Roth,
as told to Irene Burk Harrell

Super Prayerables

To Add a Glow to your Life

Irene Burk Harrell

Acton House, Inc.
Publishers

Los Angeles, California

Designed by Nancy Bundy
Manufactured in the United States of America
Composition by Freedmen's Organization
Jacket design and illustrations by Fred Hartson
Manufactured by Kingsport Press

Scripture quotations are taken from the King James Version of the Bible unless otherwise identified:
NIV = The New International Version
TAB = The Amplified Bible
TLB = The Living Bible
Williams = The New Testament in the Language of the People

Several meditations are taken from The Upper Room Disciplines, *1975, and are used by permission of The Upper Room, Nashville, Tennessee.* The Upper Room Disciplines *is an annual publication of devotions for daily use.*

ISBN 0-89202-012-1

To our growing family—

Tommy and Sue

Alice

Dino

Susan and Jimmy

'Guerite

Maria

Preface

Some might think it strange to find the name of God intermingled with the ordinary things of life which are recounted in these pages of prayerables. This book is not for them. For myself, I have finally come to know that Jesus is Lord of all of my life—or none of it, and I choose to let Him be Lord of all.

Thomas à Kempis wrote that when our hearts are right, *everything* contains a holy teaching. My prayer then is, "Create in me a right heart, O God, and teach me. Open my eyes, Lord, wider and wider, until the day when I shall see You as You really are and know even as I am known."

Contents

Such a Day	3
On Origins	5
And God Saw That . . .	7
Forty Cents Off	9
Great Expectations	11
ECU Campus	13
Band-Aids and Brokenness	15
The Greatest Show on Earth?	17
On Being Agreeable	19
Cookies, Anyone?	21
Science Fair	23
On the Pier	25
Frank Died	27
My Grandfather's Funeral	29
The Fat of the Land	31
Open-Minded	33
Dogwood Day	35
Eyes to See	37
A New Tooth	39
Warts Away	41
Fragile Beauty	43
Phew!	45
On Bats	47
No Respecter of Persons	49
Trusting God in *All* Things	51

The Cost of Living—and Loving 53
One Why of Sickness 55
Sunny Side Up 57
The News 61
Money Matters 63
"Justice" 65
Ma Died 69
Memories of Ma 71
Decisions, Decisions . . . 73
Happy Valentine's Day 75
Declaration of Independence—and Interdependence 79
Wedding Tears 81
"My son, my son" 83
The Beauty of It All 87
Sounds of Love 89
The Eye of the Beholder 91
Maria's Prayer 93
The Weeds Need Us 95
A Gray Squirrel 97
Beauty Born of Love 99
At the Beach 101

Super Prayerables

To Add a Glow to your Life

Lord I AM
thank You for the willingness
that You impart to us
thank You for opening
our eyes today.

I do know one thing: I was blind but now I see!
John 9:25 NIV

11-1-74
Such a Day

It was such a day
as there had never been
in all the history
of the world
or so it seemed to me.
The grass was greener
the sky more blue
the pines were taller
the birds sang sweeter
than ever they had before.
And I was there
right in the midst of it
savoring the sound
feasting my eyes
apprehending it all.

O God
How is it
that You open my eyes
to brand-new beauty
never before seen
created just for me
that was there all the time
waiting
for everybody?

Oh, might I show the world!

BUT ONLY *I AM* CAN SHOW THEM
ONLY *I AM* CAN OPEN EYES
WHEN *THEY* ARE WILLING.

Lord, I myself am unable to express any more appropriate reaction to the intricate marvel of Your creation. Indeed, Lord, Wow! *Amen.*

I will praise thee; for I am fearfully and wonderfully made; marvellous are thy works; and that my soul knoweth right well.
Psalm 139:14

On Origins

Our hard-of-hearing nine-year-old was home from the Central Institute for the Deaf for her Easter vacation. The old mother cat had given birth to her umpteenth litter just a few weeks earlier. Three little gray/black balls of fuzz had their eyes open, but just barely. 'Guerite was sitting on the carport steps admiring the squirming mass as the little ones nuzzled into the mama's underside and pumped her belly with their front paws. From her delighted fascinated watching, it was plain that new baby kittens were high on 'Guerite's list of the most wonderful things in God's creation. Breaking her entranced absorption in them for a moment, 'Guerite turned to me with a questioning look.

"Baby kittens cost a lot of money?" she asked.

"No," I told her, and tried to think how to explain the marvel of birth in words she could understand. Remembering that she had seen roundly pregnant women and known that a baby was growing inside them, I said, "The mama kitty got fat, and the baby kitties came out." She nodded, but that wasn't the end of it.

"Mama kitty go to hospital?" she wanted to know.

"No," I said, groping for a simple explanation. "People mamas do that"—I pointed to myself—"but not mama kitties. The mama kitty stayed at home."

Nodding again, she had another question ready. "How?" she asked, arching her back to push her stomach out. "Spit up?" She pretended to upchuck.

"Oh, no," I said. "They came out between her legs—under her tail."

'Guerite stared at me in fascinated wonderment and closed the conversation.

"Wow!" she said.

Thank You, Lord, that storms come—and go. But that You're there—before, after, and in the midst of them. Thank You, Lord, for that.

I will never leave thee nor forsake thee.

Hebrews 13:5

And God Saw that It Was Good

The first stones hit
and bounced and rolled
across the asphalt
Hail
out the airport window
Then the rain
gushed with it
and wild winds
blew wild waters
over the field
mirroring turbulent skies
the water leaping up
as fountains of welcome
to the hail
driving
thrusting its way in
Moments later
the asphalt
shining wet
a few puddles
and on the horizon
fleecy blue
below the ragged fringe
of peaceful
floating
leftover
stormcloud

Thanks, Lord, for showing me over and over and over again that saving for a rainy day is not part of Your plan for me. You give me such abundance when I live in the now and trust You for all my needs. Let me learn my lesson so well that I will share all I have with others—because it really all belongs to You anyhow. Keep giving me daily *my daily bread. Thanks, Lord.*

"Do not worry, saying, 'What shall we eat?' or 'What shall we drink?' or 'What shall we wear?' For the pagans run after all these things, and your heavenly Father knows that you need them. But seek first his kingdom and his righteousness, and all these things will be given to you as well. Therefore do not worry about tomorrow, for tomorrow will worry about itself."

Matthew 6:31-34 NIV

Forty Cents Off

I think I'll quit cluttering my billfold with cents-off coupons. I'm tired of the endless, fruitless shuffle through them at the checkout counter. The invariable result is disappointment. It was always last week that I bought the giant economy size the coupon was good on—only I forgot about it at the time. Cereal coupons are inevitably for the kind the kids don't like. And the soap coupons are for the brand much more expensive—even with discount—than the kind we prefer.

Last week, however, I thought I had it made. I bought the right kind of coffee—the kind we liked, the kind I had a 40-cents off coupon for—and I pulled the coupon triumphantly from the bulging alphabetized collection in my billfold (there was no room left for money if I'd had any) just as the checker had her hand on the coffee can.

Suddenly, triumph died. I could almost hear the coupon cackle with demonic glee as the expiration date leered up at me, a week too late.

How like our promises, Lord—so flighty, so impractical, impossible, so unkept.

But Your promises—always delivered exactly on time according to the covenant: eternal life, new creaturehood, loving kindness that lasts forever.

O, Lord, I appreciate all *that. Thank You, Lord.*

The Lord is not slack concerning his promise.

II Peter 3:9

I will sprinkle clean water upon you, and ye shall be clean. . . . A new heart also will I give you, and a new spirit will I put within you: and I will take away the stony heart out of your flesh, and I will give you an heart of flesh. And I will put my spirit within you, and cause you to walk in my statutes, and ye shall keep my judgments, and do them. And ye shall dwell in the land that I gave to your fathers; and ye shall be my people, and I will be your God.

Ezekiel 36:25-28

Great Expectations

I taped it to my study wall, and it hung there until it was dog-eared, one of my favorite pieces of advertising:

"You promised to fly her to the moon on gossamer wings. Now you have to tell her you can't swing the beach—."

And there she stood, the girl/woman to whom the promise was made, now a pouty, woebegone housefrau, too young to have a runny-nosed baby propped on one hip, an anemic little girl with stringy hair clinging stickily to her other leg. Around them was the peanut butter and jelly and dirty laundry debris of a hole-in-the-wall kitchen. The glamour of romance was gone, the glum reality of life remained.

Lord, I don't think this is quite what Your servant had in mind when he wrote, "There is neither male nor female, for ye are all one in Christ Jesus."

But this is what we've seen, everywhere we've looked, for several years. And many of my generation have wagged their heads and clucked in dire disapproval. Oh, bless them, Lord, and set them free from the unjoy of condemnation.

How I praise You that You've used all this for Your glory. Why, You've delivered us from judging by externals. You've revealed the lie of "Clothes make the man." You've given us to hold precious our bearded sons, our blue-jeaned daughters, and all their friends.

I know the day will come when styles will change again. But let our style of looking at persons remain free to keep seeing You in their faces no matter what their bodies wear.

The Lord seeth not as man seeth; for man looketh on the outward appearance, but the Lord looketh on the heart.

I Samuel 16:7

ECU Campus

Everywhere:
  wire-rimmed spectacles
  middle-parted swinging hair
  bicycles and bookbags.
Bosoms and beards distinguish,
Blue-jeaned bottoms merge
  this sexed humanity.
Brains?
  Oh, they're here too—
  It's just that you can't tell
    by looking anymore.

Lord, how often people invent an illness because they imagine the remedy is better than perfect health and wholeness. I've seen kids faking sprained ankles in order to get a turn at the crutches of a neighbor boy with a real broken leg. And all the small fry in our end of town used to sport ripped-sheet slings when one of them had a genuine broken arm.

Lord, am I like that, too? Do I ever unwittingly feign unwholeness to get out of doing something that requires able-bodiedness?

I suspect it's true—and awful! If I can have either one or the other—excuses or wholeness—but never both at once, Lord, lead me to choose the better portion, the one that fits Your will for my life. Thanks, Lord.

Wilt thou be made whole?

John 5:6

Band-Aids and Brokenness

Maria was coming downstairs after her nap. "Mama, my leg hurts," she whimpered.

"Well, I wonder why," I said, not knowing of any recent injury.

"Because I want a Band Aid," she announced, telling the whole truth.

Lord, I can remember when it was such a thrilling thing to go to the circus—or to the state fair—or almost anywhere. Now, I'd almost always rather not go. The things of the world don't have the appeal for me that they did once. Why, even Gone with the Wind *was ordinary the last time I saw it. My appetite for the world is jaded—having seen it once, I've seen it all.*

But the things of Your *creation, Lord! How I hunger to see more of them! You've blessed me with a prodigious appetite for Grand Canyons, and brand-new kittens, for ocean shores and spring showers, for mountains ablaze with autumn maples, and homebound mornings gray with fog. Don't let me ever become sated with the splendors You have made. Or with the wonder of Yourself.*

Fire and hail, snow and vapours, stormy wind fulfilling his word, mountains and all hills, fruitful trees, and all cedars, beasts and all cattle, creeping things and flying fowl . . . praise the name of the Lord, for his name alone is excellent; his glory is above the earth and heaven.

Psalm 148:8-10, 13

The Greatest Show on Earth?

"I've never seen the sun"
  shrieked the sallow complexions
    of circus youth
      selling peanuts, popcorn, chewing gum.
"There's been a water shortage"
  proclaimed the unwashed pachyderms
    synchronized in ponderous rhythm
      reeking of eau de latrine—

But the tigers looked beautiful, the trapeze artists daring. We had seen the circus for another year. It was more than enough to last for a while.

You've suggested it in Your word, haven't You, Lord? "Agree quickly with your adversary." Lord, that sounds like such *a good idea. Remind me of it the next time I'm hellbent in the opposite direction. And You've made a fantastic promise about what You will do for us whenever we agree about what we want to ask for. Please make us agreeable. Thanks, Lord.*

If two of you shall agree on earth as touching any thing that they shall ask, it shall be done for them of my Father which is in heaven.

Matthew 18:19

On Being Agreeable

A pair of people very dear to me were engaged in an almost heated discussion.

"Our guide could speak six languages," he said, telling me about their recent European trip.

"Seven," she put him down.

His glance would have incinerated a cigar-store Indian to smouldering ashes.

"Six *besides English*," he went on.

Their conversation brought home to me the sickness of our so wanting to be right that we make up new ground-rules to fit our version of truth as we go along. And it set me to wondering what would happen if these two—and I—and all others—would try as hard, work as diligently and devotedly, to agree as we do to disagree.

Lord, I wonder. I know some beautiful—in You—thin people. I know some beautiful—in You—roundish people. And I can't see that You condemn either kind. You just keep on loving us so much, no matter what.

Give us Your sense of priorities, Lord. Take our minds off ourselves, our size altogether, and rivet our attention on Yourself and Your love for us. In Jesus' name.

Behold, what an incredible quality *of love the Father hath bestowed upon us, that we should be called the sons of God. . . . Yes, dear friends, we are already God's children . . . and we can't even imagine what it is going to be like later on. But we do know this, that when he comes we will be like him, as a result of seeing him as he really is.*

I John 3:1 KJV, roman TAB
I John 3:2 TLB

Cookies, Anyone?

I wasn't there, but I heard about it afterward. It was a small social gathering, and some beautiful homemade cookies were being passed around. The rather famous lady, who was a little plumpish, looked at them longingly, said, "You know, I really shouldn't," and passed them on.

One of the young men present helped himself to a handful and challenged her with a kindly, "How old are you, Agnes?"

"Seventy-five," she said.

"Seventy-five? At your age, do you think it *really* matters?"

I don't know for sure, but I think she took a cookie.

It's hard for me to know how to react to such a sequence of events, Lord. Something in me wants to laugh, and something in me wants to cry. What's the lesson we're to learn, Lord? That enemies will find a way to overcome barriers put up by man, and one will conquer all, the weak being consumed by the strong? Or is it to set a longing in us for that new heaven and new earth where foxes and chickens can be friends? Well, thanks Lord, that I don't have to know the answer to this or to any other of life's perplexities. Thanks that it's enough to know that You *are all-knowing. It would probably be too much for me anyhow. Thanks, Lord, that You work all things together for good whether we understand or not. And thanks for the promise of heaven.*

The wolf and the lamb shall feed together, and the lion shall eat straw like the bullock; and dust shall be the serpent's meat. They shall not hurt nor destroy in all my holy mountain, saith the Lord.

Isaiah 65:25

Science Fair

There was a science fair in a classroom in one of our area elementary schools. Among the exhibits were the pets that some of the children had brought from home. They included a goldfish in a bowl, a hamster in a cage, a few yellow biddies in a box, and a live and lively red fox a farmer had caught in a trap.

Under their well-trained teacher, the children learned so much from observing the science-fair creatures at school the first day, they agreed to leave their live exhibits in the classroom overnight so they could study them the next day, too.

The decision resulted in catastrophe.

No one knew how he managed it, but somehow during the night, the fox escaped from his enclosure and enjoyed a three-course midnight snack—fish, fowl, and hamster.

What instinctual wisdom You've planted in Your creatures, Lord. I marvel. Freedom, Lord. You bought mine at such a price. Don't let the entanglements of life trap me into bartering a moment of it away. In Jesus' name.

Where the Spirit of the Lord is, there is freedom.

II Corinthians 3:17 NIV

Stand fast therefore in the liberty wherewith Christ hath made us free, and be not entangled again with the yoke of bondage.

Galatians 5:1

On the Pier

Like a baby crying
  the seagull caught
    in the fisherman's line.
Reeled in
  and untangled and untangled and untangled
offered a fish
  the gull chose freedom
    and flapped away.

I shouldn't be embarrassed, should I, Lord? I was too young to know anything of life, much less death. And I had hardly heard of You at all. And Lord, remembering all this, I see how immature I was then; and yet how I expect maturity of my children now. I'm not properly focused at all on what they ought to be, am I? Why, my seven-year-old would be more mature about death—and about many other things—than I was at twice her age.

Thanks, Lord, that You have ways of growing us up and showing us where we've been and where we've come. Lord, mature us who have the age for it, and let us rejoice that little children are little children. Let them keep on being little children until it's time for them to be something else. Thanks, Lord.

To everything there is a season, and a time to every purpose under heaven: A time to be born, and a time to die . . . .

Ecclesiastes 3:1-2

Frank Died

Eleven years old, I was visiting at the farmhouse home of my best girlfriend when my father came to get me.

"Frank died," he said.

There was only one Frank in my life, my mother's father, who lived in Michigan. I had spent many a happy summer playing in his haymow, jumping in the vast stores of grain stored loose in wooden bins, and helping to serve the enormous dinners that my grandmother—Ma, as we called her—and my aunts always prepared for the threshers.

Frank hadn't been sick, Papa said. He'd come in from the field for dinner, sat down in the rocking chair, and just left his body sitting there.

Frank had been part of my summers for as long as I could remember, and now he wouldn't be anymore. As I stood up to go home with my father, I giggled.

"Well, I guess I won't be seeing you for a little while," I said to my girlfriend.

Over the years, remembering my silly giggles at the first death I'd ever known, I've been embarrassed about it.

It's strange to me, Lord, the things that hang in our minds. But I like remembering these things that happened when Frank went to his long home. It makes me wish I had really known him and that I could remember more.

I understand from what the scientists say that all the rest of that long-ago time is stored somewhere in the computer of my brain, too, and that maybe someday I'll be able to look at it all again. I can't imagine any more interesting program for any of us than to get to see our lives sometime—the parts that are all right with us—to find out what kinds of persons we were on the way to becoming what we are now.

Life—all of it—is so interesting, Lord, the good and the bad. I'd like to live from now on so I wouldn't be ashamed of any of it. Could You make that possible for me? Wow, Lord. That would really *be new-creaturehood, wouldn't it? I'm so glad You are a God of miracles and that nothing is too hard for You.*

All things are possible with God.

Matthew 19:26 NIV

My Grandfather's Funeral

I don't remember much about the trip to Michigan for the funeral. I don't even know how many of the eight in our family went, but I suppose Papa drove and Mama sat in the front seat beside him. Three hundred sixty miles was a long way in those days when forty miles per hour seemed like flying.

I think we stopped at some department store on the way, probably in Grand Rapids, Michigan, so Mama could buy a black dress. Her face was puffy from crying and from her being kind of round that year, but beautiful as always. All I can remember of the funeral is that I sat beside Freda, Frank's youngest daughter—my mother's youngest sister—and we both cried. Whenever Freda's sobs got a little bit quiet, mine revved up. When mine would die down, hers would crescendo.

The ride home afterward? I've forgotten that, too, except that Mama still had on her new black dress, with its lace-edged white collar, and she was so uncomfortable in her too-tight girdle that she struggled to wriggle out of it while she sat in the front seat. I was kind of embarrassed, mildly shocked that she'd take off her girdle in front of Papa.

Oh, but I was talking about diets, wasn't I? Well, in the little interval of privacy that granddaddy required to shed his outer clothes and get settled in his bed, I stood in the kitchen, leaning against the sink. After modesty had been duly honored, I would get back to work. While I waited, I happened to remember the two pieces of fried chicken that had been left over from supper. Almost involuntarily, I found myself gnawing away at them, eating skin and all, sucking the bone ends clean. Nothing would do then but to top the chicken off with a heaped-up spoonful of ice cream. If my search of the refrigerator had uncovered a sugar-laden soft drink, I'd have succumbed to that, too.

All my life I've operated on the theory that the calories I consume standing up don't count. But as yet, I've been unable to prove it to my scales.

It's a funny thing about me, Lord, and I don't understand it, how practically any excuse will do for stuffing myself. Now that granddaddy is tucked in, and I'm back at my typewriter, and my husband has come home, I'd love to go out for a knock-down drag-out steak supper with all the trimmings. Only I'm tired of the trimmings being so obvious on me.

. . . .

Thanks, Lord, for giving me a glimmering just now of where some of my basic trouble lies. As long as I'm giving, pouring out of myself—whether it's words to share with others, or ministry that leaves no time for eating—I'm immune to the allurements of excessive food. But when I stop giving, I don't go into neutral—there seems to be no such gear in me—I go into reverse, and start suctioning up more than I've ever sent forth. Mercy! But thanks, Lord, for telling me. It's true, isn't it? Deeply true. I've needed to know that about myself for a long time. Now teach me to implement it to Your glory.

Remember the words of the Lord Jesus, how he said, It is more blessed to give than to receive.

Acts 20:35

The Fat of the Land

I'd have done all right with my diet today, except— There I was in the study, the clock crowding ten-thirty, food the farthest thing from my mind as I typed away excitedly on the manuscript for a new book. The little kids were tucked in bed, one big kid off baby-sitting, another touring Europe, two others entering a surfing contest at the ocean, my husband at a meeting that would likely last until the wee hours—and my mind was in full gear for creativity. But then I heard granddaddy wandering around in the kitchen. Any time he got out of his rocking chair at that time of the evening, it meant that he had disposed of his last tobacco cud for the day and was looking on the kitchen counter for his mineral oil and a glass for a last drink of water. He wanted to go to bed.

I left my desk to pull out the hideabed in the living room for him. There was no door between my study and the living room, just a double-wide archway, making the two rooms one, but granddaddy never minded my working after he had crawled between the sheets. I think he rather liked it, really, the sound of someone else close by in the house. And I had graduated to the point where I was blessed by his presence, too. I felt just as free to clatter away on the typewriter as if he hadn't been there at all.

Yes, Lord, I am the mother, the daughter is mine. Your Word tells us that we are wonderfully made—I'll take your Word for that, and I won't presume to fathom the mysteries of my own mind. But Lord, I wonder at the why of this double-mindedness in me. How come it's there? I know that a double-minded man is unstable and can't expect to receive anything from God. And I don't want to be in that position—ever—because I always need Your blessings.

. . . .

Oh! Yes, Lord. Asking You, I suddenly see it. Every double-mindedness in me is the direct result of my taking my mind off You and putting it on the circumstances. Lord, heal me of this—forever and ever—that I might be single-minded, with You always foremost in my mind. Thank You, Lord.

Thou wilt keep him in perfect peace, whose mind is stayed on thee: because he trusteth in thee.

Isaiah 26:3

Open-Minded

Her daughter's scheduled surgery was minor—
  routine repair of an injured knee
And the mother knew it.
The scheduled surgeon was sober—
  experienced, and fully competent
And the mother believed it.
The daughter was in perfect health—
  all the pre-op tests confirmed it.
And mother and daughter loved each other
  and shared firm faith
    in a living, powerful God.

When green-coated attendants
  wheeled the drug-drowsed daughter
    off to the OR suite
The mother waited
  rehearsing survivors
    for the obituary
  and debated whether the casket
    should be open or closed.

After a while
  the doctor stuck his head in the door
    "All went well," he said.
And after a longer while
  attendants wheeled the daughter back to her room
And the mother was shocked
  at how pale she looked.
Still later
  when her daughter awoke
    and spoke of pain
  the mother was surprised
    that she hurt.

Thanks, Lord. Wouldn't it be wonderful if our recollection of every day was just of the beauty of it?

. . . .

Oh! No, it's needful for us to remember pain, too, isn't it?—for whatever beautiful may come of it later. Your Word promises that You make everything beautiful in its time, and we can't pull up the tares—that seem unbeautiful—without risking destroying the beautiful along with them. And so my proper response to loveliness—and to un*loveliness—has to be to give thanks—in everything! Praise God!*

In everything give thanks, for this is the will of God in Christ Jesus concerning you.

I Thessalonians 5:18

Dogwood Day

A note that would have been in my diary had I been keeping one, was scrawled instead on a slip of paper and dropped into a box on my desk. It read simply, "April 11, 1974, Wilson, N.C. A warm day, when the sweetness of the dogwood filled the air—and fell on me."

I don't remember anything else about that day, but as I reread the jotted-down words, I smell the dogwood afresh, feel its scent upon my arms, and see the ivory purity of its blossoms.

Thanks, Lord, for answering so quickly. I do understand something now, not all of it, but something. I understand that, at my worst, my ugliest, my most hateful, I am infinitely uglier than that malformed boy. I am *uglier in Your sight—and would be in the sight of the world if they could see my heart. And one day everything about us will be seen, and known, won't it, Lord? Everybody will know that my sinfulness, my ugliness, has been willful. But that boy can't help how he is, and so he'll be one of the beautiful angels in the twinkling of an eye. Nobody will blame him.*

Lord, keep me reminded that You look not on the outward appearance but on the heart. And make me live as if I'm aware, all the time, that You're looking at a fully exposed me. Make me want to be as beautiful inside as I want to be outside.

And Lord, O most merciful Lord, plant so much of Your love in us for Your broken children that we can be channels of Your wholeness to them—in the here and now.

For now we see through a glass, darkly; but then face to face. Now I know in part, but then shall I know even as also I am known.

I Corinthians 13:12

Eyes to See

"Birds make me feel weird," Alice said, "because they have only two legs—no arms."

"How's that?" I asked, thinking birds were rather perfectly designed to do bird things.

"I'd feel helpless," she said.

Ah so. And how often I've looked at other people and thought them poorly designed or inadequately equipped for life because their equipment was not quite the same as mine—a mind not as agile, limbs less spry—. But then, their job isn't the same as mine, either. They don't *need* the same things I need.

"Birds seem to fulfill their niche perfectly well without arms, Alice. They lay their eggs, care for their nestlings, and fly south for the winter. What would they use arms for if they had them? Arms on birds would be so much superfluous baggage in flight. After all, they don't need to carry packages like we do."

It's marvelous, Lord, simply marvelous, that You've made each of us exactly right to do what we are supposed to do! Thanks, Lord.

But Lord, how about that boy, the boy I got the barest glimpse of in the shopping-center parking lot today? The boy two females were pulling and pushing along. His head was put on awry, and his neck and his lolling-out tongue were so thick and ugly, his eyes hardly alive. Lord, I wanted to cry when I saw him. I wanted them to hide him somewhere, not have him out in the open for anybody to stare at. His very presence was an obscene scrawl on Your creation. I was glad my little girl was looking the other way and didn't see him and ask unanswerable questions. It hurt, Lord. How am I to understand that? How am I to give thanks, to praise You for that?

Lord, sometimes I've caught myself wishing that spiritual growth was that automatic. But just as a plant has to have water and sun, I've found that faith has to have its nourishment, too. And partaking of the nourishment of Your Word, prayer, and grace, are more than means to an end—they are the very things that enrich life in the process. I'm glad You've made them not optional but essential to our spiritual growth. How poor life would be without them. Thanks, Lord.

Be filled with the Spirit. Speak to one another with psalms, hymns and spiritual songs. Sing and make music in your heart to the Lord, always giving thanks to God the Father for everything, in the name of our Lord Jesus Christ.

Ephesians 5:18-20 NIV

A New Tooth

Our nine-year-old daughter was proud that she had lost a tooth and that another was already poking through her gum to take its place.

"My teeth are growing up!" she said.

She lowered her magnifying eyepiece to working position as I stuck out my hand, prepared for the worst etiology in the medical encyclopedia—in all of medical history, for that matter.

"Warts," she said perfunctorily, "just warts. You can follow the same treatment."

Warts? My relief—I probably wouldn't lose my arm after all—was tempered with mortification. Warts were all right for kids—or men folks—but for me—at forty-seven? Mercy!

When I applied the formaldehyde that night—generously with a cotton swab instead of sparingly with a toothpick according to the doctor's instructions—lightning hot pain shot through my arm. It'll ease off in a little while, I told myself through clenched teeth, and crawled into bed, smothering the arm under my pillow. But apparently the pain didn't need air to thrive—it multiplied and multiplied until I could bear it no longer. Leaping from the bed, I rushed to the bathroom, stuck my hand under a faucet, filled the sink with cold water, and prayed like crazy. Warts or no warts, I wouldn't try the treatment again.

For some reason, the formaldehyde wasn't painful to Susan. She stayed with the prescribed treatment faithfully, day after day.

In a few weeks, her warts were gone. And suddenly—mine were, too.

God's healing, I decided, can work with or without medicine.

Thanks, Lord. Thanks for everything. But P.S.—I have a new crop of warts—left hand, this time. How about healing them, too? In the meantime, I will praise You, warts and all.

I am the Lord that healeth thee.

Exodus 15:26

Warts Away

Susan's warts hadn't bothered her until she fell in love. But when she started to wear her boyfriend's class ring, then it was only natural that she'd want her hands to look pretty instead of bumpy with the warts that blossomed prolifically on most of her fingers and both of her thumbs. She didn't say anything to me about them at first, but tried wrapping them tightly in adhesive tape at night to soften them and gnawing them off in the daytime, spreading the virus profusely. Inevitably, the net result was a more abundant bouquet of warts.

In despair about her backward progress, Susan mentioned her warts to me, feeling guilty that she was getting impatient for them to go away, wanting to get on with it and not have to keep waiting for God to take them away all by Himself. She'd asked Him already, it turned out.

I made an appointment for Susan with the dermatologist.

The doctor showed her how to apply a formaldehyde solution at night and castor oil in the daytime and told her to come back in a few weeks for a recheck.

I had a skin problem, too, a strange one that was becoming increasingly painful and distressing to me. While Susan and I were in the office, I asked the doctor to look at my right hand to see if I should make an appointment with her or some other kind of specialist. I explained how my ailment had begun with painful nails, making my fingers very sensitive to the slightest touch. One of the sensitive places had grown out to reach the end of the nail, where it had become an exposed and open sore that bled a lot and wouldn't heal.

Secretly, I had been imagining all sorts of dire diagnoses—had even wondered if it would be necessary to amputate my whole arm, and if so, whether or not I could learn to make corrections on galleys—part of my duties as an editor—legibly with my left hand. I didn't tell that to the doctor, of course, just gave a brief chronology of the mysterious symptoms that had me baffled and concerned.

O, thank You, gracious Lord, for all the fantastic beauty You set about us. Thank You that I can't save maple leaves or sunsets or daisies forever. Thank You that I don't have to settle for faded, leftover, remembered beauty. Every day, every moment when my heart is right, You show me something fresh and new—more beautiful than anything ever before. Hallelujah, Lord. Hallelujah!

He has made everything beautiful in its time; He also has planted eternity in men's heart . . . .

Ecclesiastes 3:11 TAB

11-21-68
Fragile Beauty

Our maple dropped its leaves last night.

This morning it stood
  with a rose-orange whorl
    of flaming petticoats
      around its ankles.
I gathered a white ironstone platterful
  of the crisp glow
  and carried it to the kitchen
    to keep forever.
But the glow frizzled and curled
  like thin meat seared in a too-hot pan.

Fragile beauty's not for taming—
I'll know, next time.

That's how it is with all our hypocrisies, isn't it, Lord? Anything we try to cover up is made worse, more blatantly obvious. We didn't even need Watergate to teach us that. Oh, so cleanse us of all our wickedness that we won't think we have to try to hide anything.

I was afraid, because I was naked; and I hid myself.

Genesis 3:10

Nothing in all creation is hidden from God's sight. Everything is uncovered and laid bare before the eyes of him to whom we must give account.

Hebrews 4:13 NIV

Phew!

One of us had picked up a new brand of bathroom deodorant at the grocery store. It was a daintily packaged rosebud floral spray that invitingly promised "a delicately refreshing aroma." We used it only once. It left our tiny bathroom reeking like a gigantic funeral parlor.

O, Lord, the wonder of life and death, and how sheltered we are from it—that even a dead bat tears at our heartstrings. I've wondered how it could be to visit places I've read about and seen pictures of—where millions are dying of starvation, or where dead soldiers are piled like cordwood on trucks for burial. What would seeing that do to me?

What does it do to You, Lord, who know *the end from the beginning? How You must cry, "O Jerusalem, Jerusalem," over us. How You must long to return, that love might rule on earth, that abundance—and not famine—might be everywhere—that nothing might hurt or destroy on all Your holy mountain. O Lord, please hurry. Let that day come soon! In Jesus' name.*

Behold, I come quickly.

Revelation 22:7

On Bats

It was after dark when Tommy came in cradling something warm and soft in his hands. He went first to show it to his brother, Dino, and I heard them marveling over it, so I stuck my head in to see what it was about. Tom had been standing out in the street, he said, in front of the house, when he caught a glimpse of something fast in the air overhead. Then he heard the soft whomp of the something as it flew into the surf racks on top of his van. Reaching up, he had found the little reddish brown bat, still warm, but dead from the impact.

He laid the bat on a paper towel on the table.

"You don't get to see them often, up close like this," he said. Both boys stroked the softness of its fur, stretched its "real neat" wings to marvel at the velvet of the webbing skin, and examined its feet, the hooks by which it hung upside down to sleep. We talked about the marvelous variety of God's creation, and wondered why the bat's radar had failed him.

Examination finished, Tom said he thought he'd skin the little creature. When I shuddered, he suggested he could give it to the cats. I cringed at that, too, and Dino protested aloud.

"Why don't you just bury it in the garden?" he said.

There was some discussion then about how, after all, it *was* dead and *could* be used for meat. Surely there was nothing wrong with that. Maybe not, but our sensitivities like better to think about something rotting away, covered with soil, turning into good earth itself, than being torn apart by carnivorous teeth. The cats were middlemen we could do without. Dust to dust via earthworms was more acceptable to us.

Tommy finally relented, seeing that our Schweitzer-ian reverence for life applied also to dead bats, and took it, wrapped in toweling, to the garden for a decent burial.

very "doing all right now" is His gift, an occasion for praising him. Unbidden, my tears flowed—with the joy of His presence. I heard myself say, "In Jesus' wonderful name, Amen." As I fished in my pocketbook for a handerchief so I could see again, the man with spreading cancer walked away.

Lord, how different that man is from me. I've learned to welcome prayer when I'm "really doing all right now," but how I turn my face from You when I'm in the depths of self-misery and see no way out. I can't even look at You then, when I'm aware of my sinfulness, my unforgivingness, my resentment. Needing it so desperately, I find it impossible to ask Your pardon, Your renewing grace, Your new-creature-hood that would let me start afresh. It's as if I choose to wallow in the mire of my wretchedness a little longer.

. . . .

Oh, thank You, Lord! Suddenly I see we're not different after all, the man and I. When I met him, I was up, acknowledging You, and he was down, where I've been sometimes, instinctively knowing that sin cannot appear before a holy God.

Let us acknowledge that You've covered us both, Lord, with the blood of Your Son's righteousness. And so let us always properly come into Your presence with thanksgiving and praise, that we may be healed and made new. And Lord, bless that man with wholeness and joy!

If my people, which are called by my name, shall humble themselves, and pray, and seek my face, and turn from their wicked ways, then will I hear from heaven, and will forgive their sin, and will heal their land.

II Chronicles 7:14

No Respecter of Persons

We were at a party. Early in the evening, we were introduced to a certain man with whom we had chatted briefly before we milled away in separate directions. He had looked well, had said nothing about any illness, but later in the evening we were told that he had had surgery for a malignancy a few months ago, and while the original post-operative prognosis had sounded good, recent checkups revealed spreading trouble.

My husband and I had joined hands with our informant and quietly prayed about the situation. At the end of the evening, when we were about to leave for home, my husband asked me to wait in the hallway, and he went back to the living room where several knots of people still lingered, chatting, and asked the man if he could have a private word with him.

Agreeable, of course, showing no sign of suspecting what my husband was up to, the man followed him into the hall. Being an important person with an influential position, he might have thought we wanted to ask a favor of him, and he acted magnanimously willing to do all he could for us.

His face registered shocked surprise when they reached the hall and my husband put his hand on the man's arm and said simply, "We've just heard about your illness. Is it all right if we pray for you?"

The response was carefully matter of fact, accompanied by a slightly strained smile of make-believe confidence.

"No, thank you, I'm doing fine just now."

"Really, we'd like to pray for you," my husband persisted.

"I'd rather not—*if* you don't mind." He was clearly final, unpersuadable. The distinguished-looking successful man shrugged his arm out of contact with my husband's hand and turned to leave.

"Well, then, pray for me," I blurted. He didn't, but stood quietly as I prayed—telling God my thanksgiving and joy in acknowledging that our every breath comes from Him, that our

"Do you have a match?"

I didn't, of course, but God's purpose for me was blazing bright in her question.

I told her no and explained how I, a non-smoker who didn't like smoke, happened to be sitting in the smoking area. She told me about her teenage boys who were always after her to quit smoking. I shared with her some of our experiences with people who had wanted to quite smoking and who had trusted God to deliver them from nicotine addiction. I assured her that God would deliver her, too—if she was willing. Before we parted, we exchanged names and addresses. Later, I had a letter from the young woman:

"It has been a week today since I met you," she wrote. "It's been one week today since I've had a cigarette. Your parting words, about never having to put another one in my mouth, if I'd just ask for the Lord's help, really hit me, and I decided then to ask Him. I haven't even wanted one."

There was another letter, half a year later. Her cigarettes were still gone, and her friend's husband was back at work, good as new.

Lord, from now on, You make my seat assignments.

Let all those who trust in thee rejoice; let them ever shout for joy.

Psalm 5:11

Trusting God in *All* Things

"Smoking or non-smoking," the flight attendant assigning seats asked me when I handed her my ticket envelope.

"Non-smoking," I answered, as always, and she pulled an adhesive assignment number from her chart and stuck it on my envelope. "15C" it said.

Boarding the plane, I saw the usual "smoking permitted behind this sign" notice on row 8, and I questioned the assignment given me. It seemed to be clearly in the area where smoking was permitted. But when another non-smoker came to sit in the same area, we concluded that that flight must have an uncommonly high proportion of non-smokers. Sure enough, the area stayed free of smoke.

At the plane's first stop—not my destination—where passengers got off, the stewardess announced that non-smokers could move into the first eight rows for the next leg of the trip.

Ordinarily I'd have moved up without delay, but, somehow, I had a sense of being supposed to be where I was. But why was I to be there? I knew there was a reason and assumed it would be revealed to me. So, instead of moving up to the unpolluted area, I simply moved over to the window seat in the same row where I had occupied the aisle position.

Soon, a very attractive young woman sat down beside me. We visited a little. She was on her way to be with a friend whose husband was in the hospital—intensive care unit—with a massive heart attack. *Ah ha!* I thought. *That's the reason I stayed put.* When I began to question her about her relationship to Jesus and whether or not she knew His healing power was available today just as it was when Jesus walked the earth as a man, I learned that she was already a turned-on Christian and that many Spirit-filled prayer groups had been alerted to pray for her friend.

Well, that was wonderful. But I was wondering anew why I was sitting in the smoking area. Surely she didn't need me to witness to her. Then it came.

After rummaging in her purse for a moment, she asked,

O, Lord, thank You! Thank You for waking my understanding to such truth. If I hold sugar "dear" because I paid all of ninety cents a pound for it, how much more dear I am to You—who paid Your very life for me!

Lord, remind me of that if ever I'm depressed again, if ever I believe the lie that nobody cares about me. Lord, emblazon the fact of my preciousness to You, my dearness to You, so upon my mind that feelings of loneliness, unwantedness, can never again be part of my life. Let me continually affirm how ineffably much You love me—

And Lord, let grow in me that kind of love, that kind of precious regard for all my neighbors, the whole world over. Renew in me Your mind, that sees each one as of infinite value, bought with greater love hath no man than this—

For ye are bought with a price: therefore glorify God in your body, and in your spirit, which are God's.

I Corinthians 6:20

A new commandment I give unto you, That ye love one another, as I have loved you.

John 13:34

The Cost of Living—and Loving

Sugar, ninety cents a pound! The burgeoning inflation hit us in a year when two of our kids were in college, a third filling out applications for the fall semester in a non-state university, our ten-year-old in a faraway private school for the deaf. There were multifarious other expensive complications that year, too. All in all, our financial situation was almost ludicrously incomprehensible. And every week's trip to the supermarket revealed new believe-it-or-not price increases.

We began to try to economize, but after being out of sugar for a few days, I succumbed to picking up a five-pound bag—I'd always bought the ten-pound size before—took it home and carefully emptied it into the big copper canister, shaking every possible grain out of the bag. I filled the cut-glass sugar bowl only half full for the breakfast table the next morning, thinking the sugar might go further that way. Besides, there'd be less to spill.

Something I'd taken so for granted all my life had become "riches" to me. I felt blessed and privileged to have it, thankful, of course. And there was in me an almost preciousness toward the sugar because I had bought it at such a price.

Lord, I don't understand it all, but I thank You for what I do understand, and I rejoice in the love of my brethren. Thank You for all the fringe benefits of my child's temporary indisposition. Maybe, someday, I'll be the kind of person who will keep in touch with friends, who will go to see somebody just for a visit, not for a purpose, and You won't have to crowd me into it. Until then, Lord, until then, I'll praise You for how it is now.

Two are better than one, for they have a good reward for their labor; for if they fall, the one will lift up his fellow. But woe to him that is alone when he falleth; for he hath not another to help him up.

Ecclesiastes 4:9-10

One Why of Sickness

Maria had been sick for several days. We had prayed, trusting the Lord to heal her—but she wasn't getting any better as far as we could see. Because of certain engagements on my calendar for the next week, I needed to have her back in school on Monday, so I reluctantly made an appointment and took her to the doctor. We had gotten to know Dr. Ryburn, a local pediatrician, during the years when our toddlers were forever having shots for this, that, and the other. It was good to see him again.

After a brief examination, he told us exactly what Maria's sickness was, and prescribed medicine that would clear it up promptly.

On the way home, I stopped by the drugstore to have the prescription filled. Heading for the store, I was not fussing, not asking any complaining "why?" but just wondering why Maria hadn't already gotten well by God's sovereign action in answer to our prayers.

As I shoved open the door and greeted the druggist—our friend from years of much medicine—I was flooded with the revelation that God in His wisdom and mercy has planned for us to love one another, to bear one another's burdens. And how could we love Dr. Ryburn, how could we love the druggist, Grady Thomas, if we had never gotten to know them? And how could we have become acquainted even, if we hadn't had occasion to need their services?

Sunny Side Up

My sixteen-year-old gourmet was at it again. "I'm sorry, Mama," she said, getting up from the table and pouring herself a bowl of cornflkes, "but the eggs just won't do this morning. They aren't right."

Well, that was no problem to me. The eggs seldom suited her, especially if breakfast had been on the hurry-up side. And that day I needed to hurry with the clean-up after breakfast, too, in order to keep an early appointment. Boiled eggs and juice and toast breakfast was quicker to clean up after, than bacon and scrambled eggs, I'd decided long ago. And Susan's finickyness about eggs was her problem, not mine. Maybe someday she'd outgrow it.

But that day there was a further comment from another quarter.

"Your mother has a thing about boiled eggs," my husband said. "She doesn't eat 'em herself and so she doesn't like to cook 'em long enough." (I wish I could remember the exact words on paper—those don't sound cutting enough.)

That was a lie! I *do* eat boiled eggs, enjoy them too, but I wasn't having any breakfast that morning, being too wrenched with hurt and pain from overhearing the distressful ugly confrontation *he'd* had with a little one upstairs that morning. My throat was too full of lump for any kind of breakfast to find its way down. But I do know how to cook boiled eggs long enough. It was just that I'd stayed in bed too long to get the eggs in the water soon enough. The extra minutes of lying snuggled up to my husband in the cool of the morning were worth something to both of us, I'd thought. And I had put the eggs on to cook the first thing when I got downstairs and left them on until we absolutely had to have breakfast on the table right then or have everybody late for something.

Besides, it wasn't as if the eggs weren't thoroughly cooked, just that the inmost part of the yolks was kind of damp gold instead of crumbly and mealy gold as Susan liked them. Was that so great a crime? What was worst of all about it, I think, was the way my husband kind of laughed when he said it, making unkind fun of me in front of the others. A joke at my expense.

Lord, there'd be no way to describe the ugliness, the cold hate, that welled up inside of me, would there? I wanted to tell him where he could go and stay for ever. I was glad I had a good job of my own, could be self sufficient, and provide for the children, too, if necessary. He could just—

Lord, I hadn't any idea there could be such despising inside me. Why, I couldn't even love the lovable daughter who'd brought the subject up so gently, apologetically, and I certainly could never love him *again. And the little one who'd aggravated him so, starting the day off with hell instead of heaven, she could get lost too, for all I cared. Ooooh! I was almost trembling with rage when I went upstairs to bathe and dress while the family ate breakfast.*

Well, it was a superficial day, with nothing significant said between us. He might not have known, but I was seething inside. And I certainly wasn't going to say anything about it—ever. In my emotions, I ran the gamut from being determined never to serve boiled eggs ever again, to deciding to set the alarm for some ungodly early hour so I could get up in time to let the eggs cook for hours. I wound up blasé, not caring—about anything—anybody.

The day got gone, coldly stable, impersonal. He had a meeting that night, and after bathing and bedding the little people, I went up to bed at a reasonable hour to read. There was a vague awareness of a dull beginning headache as I read, but it wasn't too bad. When he came in, we talked pleasantly enough of a few inconsequential things. But as we talked, the dull beginning headache began to crescendo, and by the time he went downstairs to see about locking up, I felt myself growing pale, fierce pain claiming the total attention of my awareness. As I lay down, the pain struck. Unbearable. Hard.

When he came back up, he found me sobbing aloud, sitting up in bed, rocking back and forth with the unendurable agony of it.

He prayed for me immediately, fetched what I thought would help—a cold wet rag and a pan of ice and water so I could keep it freshly cold. When I noticed that my hands and arms were getting numb, he wanted to know if he should call the doctor, but I said no. (I wouldn't want anyone to see me like that!)

About then, the phone rang, a wonderful Christian friend who needed to talk with him—and every word of my husband's conversation on the bedside phone was a hammer bruising my brain. After a little, he asked the friend and his wife to pray for me, and they must have done it over the phone because my husband was mercifully silent, listening, whispering, "Yes, Lord," and "Thank You, Jesus" at intervals, and muttering softly some words I did not understand.

The headache was still the worst I'd ever had, but after a little, I was able to stop rocking and stop crying and lie down, shutting out the searing light with the icy rag on my eyes. The night seemed interminable, but somewhere toward morning, I slept. When I awoke, I was well.

Lord, who'd have thought half a dozen imperfectly done eggs could trigger such dangerous poison, such unforgiveness, such resentment, such pain?

Lord, when will I learn—ever?—that I can't afford to hold resentment, to harbor unforgiveness, ever, for even a second, about insults, eggs, or anything, but that in everything I must praise You? Teach me, before apoplexy takes me. Guard my lips, that I may not bring pain to another. And thank You, Lord, for forgiving me, for letting my husband forgive me, and for letting me forgive us both.

Let not the sun go down upon your wrath.

Ephesians 4:26

Lord, it's true. We're like that. Always condemning, always looking for—even gloating over the possibilities of—something less than perfection in our fellow human creatures. Why is it? Is it because we know ourselves so well—the abysses of our own imperfections—that we want imperfection recognized in others, too? Or what is it, Lord?

. . . .

Oh, yes, Lord. You understand. I don't have to. Never mind explanations then. It is *sin. Cleanse me of it. Over and over again until the thing is done. Thank You, Lord, for always looking for the best in me—and oh Lord, please make me want to look for the best in others.*

And God saw that the wickedness of man was great in the earth, and that every imagination of the thoughts of his heart was only evil continually.

Genesis 6:5

Be ye transformed by the renewing of your mind . . . so as to find and follow God's will; that is, what is good, well-pleasing to Him, and perfect.

Romans 12:2 KJV and Williams

The News

Such a shock!
Everybody whispered "suicide"
  but her doctor brother
  was the first on the scene
  and he wrote "heart attack"
  on the death certificate.

Her husband went dry-eyed about his business—
  the business of living—
The day after she was buried.
Feigned grief would have been longer,
  not to seem unseemly short
Wouldn't it?

But then
  in just a little while
  he married the girl who loved him
  and they moved away.

It was years ago
And we've finally stopped gossiping—
  unless someone just "happens" to bring it up—
But we're still wondering.

an advance of $1,000.''

Well, I wrote a letter thanking the editor who had informed us of the good news, but not until after I'd thanked the Author of the original Good News, the One whose hand was behind it all. And now I want to say it again.

Thanks, Lord. Surely You are interested in everything in our lives, the great and the small, and You demonstrate Your power and love in supplying all our needs out of Your riches in glory. And Lord, thanks that You sometimes give us a little ahead-of-time glimpse of Your provision when we need it most.

P.S. The same publisher accepted the next manuscript, too—with an even bigger advance!

Your heavenly Father knoweth that ye have need of all these things. But seek ye first the kingdom of God, and his righteousness, and all these things shall be added unto you.
Matthew 6:32-33

Money Matters

I'd never had an advance in royalties from that particular publisher before. Oh, I'd asked for one often enough, everytime I'd sent them a new book-length manuscript for consideration. But they'd always written back with some reason why they couldn't give *me* money in advance. Their reasons sounded permanent.

I was invariably disappointed, but convinced, and would sign and mail the contract to them anyhow—without an advance.

This time, however, we really needed the money *now.* I don't remember whether I asked for an advance or not when I mailed the manuscript. We had come so far in trusting God for everything. . . . And it was no lack of trust a few nights later when we were led to get on our knees, my husband and I, and not ask for, but *claim* a thousand-dollar advance on the book. I didn't know what that publisher's usual advance might be, or, in fact, if they ever gave advances to anybody, but I *knew* the thousand was mine—even though I had no natural assurance they'd even like the manuscript—they'd rejected my last one—much less accept it and go out on a limb and issue a contract with an advance.

Sure enough, a couple of weeks later, the letter came: "We like the manuscript and are prepared to issue a contract with

"Justice"

It gave me a funny feeling to open the envelope with the return address, "The Sheriff of Wilson County." I hadn't done anything illegal, as far as I knew. I understood as soon as I unfolded the sheet of paper and read: Jury Summons.

Good! I had been hoping to serve on a jury some day, to participate in one of the things that makes America great—her judicial process of speedy fair trails, by impartial juries, under rules designed to bring out the truth, to eliminate prejudice, to protect the innocent, to insure freedom from tyranny.

I learned a lot that week. When we were dismissed on Friday afternoon, I emerged from the courthouse with feet dragging, head bowed, with the conviction that our system is tremendously inefficient, woefully inadequate, and that it actively perpetuates injustice.

No defendant was wrongly convicted, but most of the guilty were set free—to have another fling at violence, larceny, drunken driving.

"It is my duty to warn you that anything you say may be held against you," seemed to have been replaced by the doctrine that a premature confession of guilt by someone caught redhanded was a practical guarantee that he'd be found "not guilty."

And something had become of the good-old-days assumption that people told the truth after they were duly sworn and put on the witness stand. Over and over again I heard conflicting evidence. Someone *had* to be lying. And yet not once was there a stern admonition from the judge, never a warning about the laws of perjury. Lying was apparently an expected part of the game.

One almost toothless juror, on being asked whether he believed in the judicial principle that a man is innocent until he is proved guilty, grinned his vacant grin more broadly and affirmed his strict adherence to this belief, adding, "Yassuh. I beliebs they'se guilty until they'se proved not guilty." Neither side excused him from serving as a juror.

Prosecutors were handsomely paid to prove a defendant guilty beyond a reasonable doubt, defense attorneys were handsomely paid to plant a reasonable doubt in the jurors' minds, a judge was handsomely paid to make sure everyone played by the rules. Female clerks were paid to get it all down in shorthand and/or on tape—but nobody was paid to discover and present all the relevant truth to the jury called to decide the case.

Rules of evidence admitted only bits and pieces of the truth, along with bits and pieces of lies.

It was a cat and mouse game. Instead of the whole truth, jurors were given a snarled web of unanswered questions, denied insinuations, a phenomenal tangle of unproven contradictions and loose ends. Many of the witnesses openly admitted that they had been intoxicated at the time of the occurrence of the events about which they were testifying. Only two defendants denied being drunk at the time of the alleged incident leading to their arrest. One woman said, "Naw. I wasn't drunk. I hadn't had nuthin' to drink 'cept beer, and you can't get drunk offen beer." Another defendant said in an indignant tone, "Me? Drunk? I wasn't drunk—I could walk—"

The lack of pertinent ballistics reports, medical records, fingerprinting, sober witnesses, and thorough investigation frustrated jurors who would honestly have liked to arrive at justice. Sometimes we probably did. Not *because* of the evidence but in spite of the lack of it. Sometimes there was a hung jury, a mistrial, and the particular cat and mouse were rescheduled to go through the same inconclusive motions again at a later date. More times than not, defendants obviously guilty in the opinion of all the jurors, were pronounced "not guilty." There was no reasonable doubt in our minds or hearts, but the evidence we were permitted to consider was not sufficient to substantiate what we knew to be true.

What's the immediate answer?

The experts tell me there is none. They explain that the law is so old, the rules so importantly complex, so tried and true, that there's no way out.

Well, obviously I'm not an expert, but there's something I'd like to suggest for starters:

1) Choose twelve good men and true who know nothing of the rules of evidence, who don't believe that defendants have any more rights than plaintiffs.

2) Closet the twelve with the accused and his accusers, with whatever documentary evidence has been collected, and with whatever witnesses they require. Let them thrash it out—sans judges, sans lawyers, sans prosecutors, sans law books, sans precedents.

3) Let them all flatfootedly, without apology, require truth from one another. No technical loopholes, no immunity from being asked relevant questions and being required to give relevant, honest answers.

4) Let them stay "in community" until there emerges a satisfied "sense of the meeting."

Who knows? Maybe the "good guys" would win once in a while. Maybe guilty defendants would come to appreciate "guilty" verdicts. One or two simple cases with truth arrived at, not just conjectured about, might do something more to start defendants happily down the road to responsible citizenhood than all the *nol-prosses, nolo contenderes,* not guiltys, and "objections sustained" in the world.

From where I sat, almost anything is worth a try.

We could call this revolutionary new system something nostalgic like "trial by a jury of your peers."

Honesty as a part of the road to justice is also based on a rather ancient principle: "Confess your sins to one another . . . that ye may be healed."

We've goofed it royally, haven't we, Lord. We've made such a mess, we can't mend it. We'll have to start over. But where can that happen? How can that happen? Where can we begin to begin again? It seems so hopeless—we can never do it.

Lord, You'll just have to do it for us! Hallelujah!

Behold, the days come, saith the Lord, that I will raise unto David a righteous Branch, and a King shall reign and prosper, and shall execute judgment and justice in the earth.

Jeremiah 23:5

Ma Died

It was a Monday morning. The four older kids had gotten off to school and my husband was ready to leave for court. I was sitting in the low platform rocker beside the hearth in the family room, holding our brand-new baby in my arms. We'd just come home from the hospital the day before, and had had a houseful of company all day. Now everybody was gone, and a peaceful day stretched before me. My husband knelt beside us—to say goodbye for the day I supposed. Instead, I heard, without preamble, "Ma died. While you were in the hospital."

"Ma" was my mother's mother. She was old, had been sick for a long time. But earlier, she had been a rich part of my life, and I had many wonderful memories. Years before, she had named my mother "Marguerite"—and the new baby in my arms was "Marguerite," too. It seemed full circle, appropriate somehow that one soul should leave when another entered this realm of earth.

I was too full to say anything, but my husband understood, brushed my cheek with a kiss, and was gone.

My tears rolled down for Ma—and her Marguerite, for my Marguerite and for me—for the mystery of birth and death.

O Lord, the joy and sorrow of life. You've made it all *so poignant, so beautiful, so rich. Thank You, Lord, that it's all forever in Your hands.*

I am persuaded that neither death nor life . . . shall be able to separate us from the love of God, which is in Christ Jesus our Lord.

Romans 8:38-39

Lord, the memories of Ma's house are so sweet to me. It's only lately that I've wondered whether or not she knew You. I know You died for us all. Lord, take care of her, too.

He is patient with you, not wanting any to perish, but everyone to come to repentance.

II Peter 3:9 NIV

Memories of Ma

My best memories of my maternal grandmother began about four o'clock on summer mornings when Papa would help Mama get all six of us kids into the family car and we'd head for Ma's house in Michigan. Papa would stay at home to go to his job every day.

The air would be deliciously cool at that hour, usually foggy. Our car was invariably in such pitiful condition that we were guaranteed several flats, steaming radiators, and broken fanbelts before midnight or so when we'd have accomplished the 360 miles and would turn into the sandy drive going up the hill to the big white house with the Weatherby red barn so grand behind it.

Mama would drive onto the grass in the backyard and park under the windmill that really worked. Someone would honk the horn, and the dog would bark, chickens might squawk, and Ma, her snowy hair in a knot on top of her head (hanging loose down her back if she'd given up on us and had gone to bed) would come running out with a loving welcome.

We'd stay a couple of weeks—eating and playing and laughing and enjoying the pump at the kitchen sink, and hot water dipped from the "reservoy" at the side of the big black wood stove in the kitchen, the kerosene lamps, and other old-fashioned wonders so much better than our Ohio modern conveniences.

Father, I thank You that there is only one Jesus. I praise You that nothing else in heaven or on earth compares with Him. Once I have settled on Him, I have the best for all eternity. And the longer I choose to choose Him, to offer myself in His name, the more certain I am that I have made not just the right choice, but the only one. Anything that might have seemed an alternative to me has long since faded away. I sing Hallelujah that He is all in all, infinite variety, just exactly what I want, and precisely what I need, all in Himself. The Perfect Everything. Father, how I praise You for the Choice You have given me. And I thank You especially, just now, for the baffling wonder, the mind-blowing mystery, that somehow, long before I knew to choose You, You had already chosen me! Amen!

. . . Choose you this day whom ye will serve. . . . I have chosen you. . . .

Joshua 24:15; John 15:16

Decisions, Decisions . . .

Walking through a large department store one day, I passed by row after row of china and glassware on display. I didn't take time to stop and examine any of it, but in the midst of the colorful array, I thought about how difficult it would be to pick the pattern I liked best from the profuse abundance there. Among so many selections, it would be difficult to choose one to prefer above all others. Pressed for a decision, I might have found myself having to eeny, meeny, miny, moe to settle upon anything.

In the past, I'd often had decisions to make about house furnishings, clothing, paint colors, appliances—almost anything you can name. Clear preferences are not always easy to come by. Some options have certain advantages, others have others. And once an irrevocable decision has been made, we've heard ourselves thinking, "Maybe I should have chosen that other pattern, it's probably more durable." Or less expensive. Or more practical. Or it would have been the wisest choice for any of a million other considerations. But we are stuck with what we have chosen whether or not we are satisfied.

Decisions, decisions . . . Choices, choices . . . Regrets, regrets . . . If onlys, if onlys . . . .

Happy Valentine's Day

I was thinking of my parents a few days before Valentine's Day and wanted to send them some special remembrance. Since I hadn't had time to do any shopping, and they lived hundreds of miles away, I decided to wire some flowers for the table. Calling a local florist, I told him what I had in mind. He gave me the approximate cost of my order, found the name of a florist in a town near where my parents live, and it was all settled. I enjoyed thinking how surprised and delighted Mama and Papa would be when they went to the door and were greeted by a messenger with a beautiful arrangement of flowers for the table.

On Valentine's Day afternoon, I telephoned my folks just to see how they were getting along. In the midst of the conversation, Mama thanked me for the flowers.

"The florist's box was in the garage when we came home from shopping for groceries," she said. "I just left them out there where they'll keep cool until I can look in the cupboard and see if I can find a vase that will be right for them."

"You mean they weren't already in a vase—arranged with fern and ribbon and all that?" I sputtered. I could hardly believe it.

"No," she said. "They were long-stemmed carnations—in a box."

I don't remember much about the rest of our conversation. I was too full of disappointment, feeling that my Valentine surprise for them had been ruined. As soon as our conversation was finished, I called the florist and told him what had happened.

"Didn't I order the right thing?" I asked him. "I just assumed that the flowers would be in a vase, all arranged—"

"Well," he stammered, "I knew that was what you wanted, but when I called the florist where your folks live— They charge so much for arranging—" He stopped apologizing and came out with it. "I just took it upon myself while I was on the telephone to tell them to send the flowers in a box. That way, they wouldn't cost so much, and there wouldn't be the expense of an extra phone call."

I didn't try to hide my indignation.

"Why, my mother can't arrange flowers any better than I can," I fumed. "She might not even have a vase that will do. The flowers will never look as right as they would if they'd been fixed by the florist."

He didn't say anything.

"And how about the other order I placed at the same time?" I wanted to know. "The flowers for our little girl in the faraway school for the deaf? She wouldn't have had a vase—"

"Oh," he said. "I don't have the order right here in front of me, but I'm sure those were arranged, all right. As I recall, their rates weren't as high as that other place—"

Yeah, he knows I won't find out about those, I figured. Only I didn't just think it. I said it out loud to one of my at-home-for-the-weekend college daughters. As soon as the words were out of my mouth, I was sorry.

"Boy, I'm sure the loving one, aren't I, Alice? Giving other people credit for the best of intentions—"

"Yeah, Mom," she agreed, accepting me anyway. Only I didn't feel so accepting of myself.

Lord, I've done and said several ugly things today. Oh, not out and out ugly like an honest pagan, but worse, in a way. I didn't bawl the florist out, exactly. He probably wishes that I had. If I had bawled him out, insisted that he redo the order as I had originally placed it, and pay for the mistake out of his own pocket, he could have defended himself somehow, made a justification satisfactory to himself about his actions. He might even have gone home and told his wife how bad-tempered that so-called Christian woman was. He'd have been poorer in his pocket, but he'd have had some self-righteousness inside to satisfy himself.

As it was, I deprived him of that, and there was no satifaction left in it for him. The action he had taken, doing the best he knew how, acting in what he felt was my best interest, too, had backfired. There was no satisfaction for anybody but the enemy who loves to set us at odds with one another.

Well, Lord, what am I to learn from this that is still rankling inside me—my own intense dissatisfaction, my guilt from heaping guilt upon the florist, my feelings about the disappointment my folks must have felt at the unarranged flowers?

Lots of things, Irene, He seems to say to me. *Lots of things. Patience, for one.* That word came through the lips of a son who had worked with a florist once.

"You know the guy's under a lot of pressure on Valentine's Day," he said.

"I'd have been disappointed, too, Mom," a daughter sympathized. "Flowers that aren't arranged—yuck. But you ought to be glad someone is watching out for you—to keep you from getting ripped off at prices that are too high."

"Noble intentions, all right," I agreed, still trying to think it through. "The florist's motive was all right, but look at what happened. Instead of having to pay a little too much for something I wanted, I wind up paying the full price for something I don't want—"

"I guess praise the Lord anyway, huh?" my son reminded me.

That was it. Only suddenly it wasn't a case of praising the Lord anyway as if it was something to be done grudgingly or against my druthers. It was—and always is to be—a positive praising of Him from whom all blessings flow. A seeing that what has happened—no matter what it is—*is* for good. And everything He can work together for good *has* to be a blessing, however we may look at it with our finite minds and our limited perspective.

The other things that passed through my mind were some thoughts about the shame of my riches, the hideousness of my pride. So rich that I could think my folks would consider a dozen miracles of red carnations from God's magnificence something of a nuisance unless they were adorned with a florist's ribbon and a container of plastic or clay. So full of sick pride I didn't want my parents—or the florist—to think I couldn't afford to send arranged flowers.

Well, Lord, I do thank You and praise You for all that happened, for all You continually show me about myself, for how far I have yet to go to live in the victory You bought for me at the price of Your life. Thank You, Lord, that You have paid it all. Grow me up so that You can show Your love through me—especially in untoward circumstances.

Thank You, Lord, that You don't leave me holding my guilt when I've done something wrong. Thank You that even when I've been *wrong with all my being, You are there, loving me, redeeming me, setting me back on a right path. O Lord, I thank You for all that. Please keep on working on me to make me like You are. Amen.*

If we confess our sins, he is faithful and just to forgive us our sins, and to cleanse us from all unrighteousness.

I John 1:9

Declaration of Independence—and Interdependence

It's never happened at my house or your house, of course, but we all understand that it happens frequently at the homes of other people. Some grownup, probably a parent, flies off the handle about something and stomps out, slamming the door, gunning the motor of the car, and screeching the brakes around the corner. The kids are left cowering in a corner and staring open-mouthed at the other authority figure for an explanation—as if *she* is on trial for *his* sin.

Or maybe the situation is that Dad has pulled a weekend drunk full of excesses of ugly talk, beating and slamming on the children, ranting and raving at the wife.

Or maybe it's something less dramatic. Maybe the old man has just made a rather unintelligent decision, not having heard all the facts of the case, and the kids are dissatisfied about it and have come running to Mama for an explanation.

The mother is at a loss. How can she justify the unjustifiable, explain the inexplicable, encourage the children to honor their father in the face of his obvious dishonorableness? How can she get them to see that the man is one thing and his actions are something else and at the same time train up the children to be accountable for what they do?

Looking around us, we see that there are no easy answers and that the same kind of problem occurs in relationships other than those having to do with domestic tranquillity. You may go out of your way to do something special to please another person and somehow the thing goes awry and what was meant to delight is received as a chastisement. What then?

No one would pretend that there is an easy answer to every problem in human relations. And the enemy would have us grovel, feeling condemned at every turn. But God Himself speaks freedom to us. As where His Spirit is, there is freedom, so it must follow that we can put away our "Woe is me" and declare our independence:

I am not responsible for the actions of other adult people. (God has made them free. And Jesus has borne the penalty. Completely.)

I am not responsible (I bear no guilt) for others' reactions to my actions when I know my heart is right before God, when I know my intentions are good. (When people are angry with me, it's *their* problem.)

But in every case, I am responsible to pray for them and for me, that God will bless us to know and do His will.

Thank You, Lord, that You bought liberty for us at such a price. Don't let us submit ourselves to the slavery of misery ever again. In Jesus' name, Amen.

If the Son therefore shall make you free, ye shall be free indeed.

John 8:36

For freedom Christ has set us free; stand fast therefore, and do not submit again to a yoke of slavery.

Galatians 5:1 RSV

Wedding Tears

I knew that people cried at weddings. I had cried myself, without understanding why. I thought it had something to do with a realization of the significance of the commitment the couple was making, a significance they couldn't begin to grasp themselves. Marriage is such a huge step, such a forever arrangement. Full of joy, full of heartache, full of fulfillment, full of disappointment. It's natural we would feel emotional, just thinking about a young couple embarking on a two-lives-made-one adventure.

I sat in church a month ago yesterday and looked at our first-born son standing up front, so handsome in gray flannel with a velveteen collar, a ruffled shirt, his neatly trimmed beard and Abe Lincoln wavy hair making him look like somebody's ancestral portrait. When the wedding march began, I turned and watched Sue glide down the aisle—oh, so beautiful, her eyes starry with tears. My eyes were wet, too, and so were Sue's mother's eyes.

And there was a gradual dawning awareness in me as I sat there, worshiping God in the wedding ceremony, that real wedding tears don't come from any soulish knowing or not knowing anything about the magnitude of the step the bride and groom are taking but *from the certain fact of the holy presence of God in our midst.* He's the one who ordained marriage—He's the one who does the joining together. And the tears are the natural overflow of the rivers of living water He has put within us.

Hallelujah, Lord, hallelujah! I'm so thankful for the abundant evidence that You were there, above all we could ask or think. Thank You for joining Tommy and Sue together in holy matrimony. Let nothing ever come between them, Lord. Let them grow together as one in You to the glory of Your name. And let Your rivers of living water, Your very own Holy Spirit, forever refresh them and keep them in Your will. In Jesus' name. Amen.

Jesus shouted to the crowds, "If anyone is thirsty, let him come to me and drink. For the Scriptures declare that rivers of living water shall flow from the inmost being of anyone who believes in me." (He was speaking of the Holy Spirit, who would be given to everyone beliving in him.)

John 7:37-39 TLB

"My son, my son"

Unintentionally
  by something thoughtless I said
    just making conversation
I had stirred the old man's memories.
And he remembered
  out loud
    the long ago day.
I could tell it still hurt
  by the sound of his voice
    and the way he kept swallowing.

"He hadn't been drunk
  in about twelve months," he said.
"And I thought
  he was probably quit.
But his wife come up to the house that night
  with the kids
  like she was aimin' to stay.
And when I ast her
  where *he* was
She kind of looked down and said,
  'Oh, I left him to home.'

" 'Drunk?' I ast her
  knowing the answer afore she said it.

"When the neighbors come to tell me
  I went to see it myself—
  the chair all burned up
And I could tell
  about how it had to happen
    from what I seen there.

"Most likely
he'd dropped a match in his lap
tryin' to light his cigarette.
His hands was all smutty
where he'd tried to put it out
And you could tell
where he'd rolled and rolled
across the floor
and touched the bed.

"He was lyin' on the floor
flat of his back
And someone had pulled a sheet
over his head.
I lifted it up—
And then I let it back down."
The old man shook his head.
"I never thought
it would be that way.
He hadn't been drunk
in about twelve months.
And I thought
he was probably quit."

I knew the man slightly, Lord, the one who died. It was such a long time ago—before I really knew You. And of course it never entered my head to tell him that You could take away the wretched wastedness of his life and give him vibrant new-creaturehood. That You could fill him so full of rivers of living water that he'd never thirst for bondage to a whiskey bottle again. No, it didn't enter my head to speak in such a way to him because I didn't know that truth myself. And so I, too, had been encouraged by what seemed less frequent drunkenness in his life.

Forgive me, Lord, that I ever rejoice—even a little bit—when anybody shows a temporary by-his-own-bootstraps improvement in anything. Let me pray the life-giving, permanent-improvement prayer for each and all instead:

"Lord, make him so miserable he can't live without You."

And Lord, heal the old man's memories. Give him to believe that Your salvation, freely given to the thief on the cross, was there for the son, who might have called upon Jesus with his last choking breath.

All that the Father giveth me shall come to me; and him that cometh to me I will in no wise cast out.

John 6:37

O Lord, we praise You for Your great power and love that made so beautiful a world for us to enjoy. Open our eyes and ears and hearts to it. Amen.

And God saw everything that he had made, and behold, it was very good.

Genesis 1:31

The Beauty of It All*

For the beauty of the earth; . . .
Lord of all, to Thee we raise
This our hymn of grateful praise.

A stately hymn! How many times I had sung it—stately! And then one day, after years of dedicated "churchianity," Jesus became real to me. Singing the same hymn, voicing the same written-down words, I was decidedly *un*stately—because my soul was rejoicing, "Jesus, I thank You and praise You for all the beautiful things You have made for me to enjoy." I felt He had made each beautiful thing for me personally.

Jesus tells us that we must become as little children to enter the kingdom of heaven, to experience the exuberant joy of the abundant life He came to bring us.

My hard-of-hearing eight-year-old has no trouble taking personally God's marvelous "good" creation. One morning recently she became aware of the sound of a bird calling outdoors, "Reet, reet," over and over again. She *knew* the bird was calling her name, "Guerite" (pronounced *greet*). There was perfect childlikeness in her as she rushed to a window, stuck her head out and called joyously back to him, "Bird, bird!"

I am certain God means for grown-ups to take every manifestation of beauty no less personally than that.

---

*Reprinted, with permission, from *The Upper Room Disciplines 1975,* © 1974 by The Upper Room, Nashville, Tennessee.

that help can get there quickly." The siren was a sound of man's caring for his fellowman. And since we can care only because God first loved us, the siren became a sound of God's love. Is anything more beautiful?

Thank You, Lord, for all the beauty of caring, and for the richness of Your promise that as we minister to the least of these, we're ministering unto You. Amen.

Beloved, if God so loved us, we ought also to love one another.

I John 4:11

Sounds of Love*

When we think about the beautiful sounds God's world has to offer, we are likely to think in terms of melodic bird songs, gurgling mountain streams, our favorite symphonies, the voice of a loved one. It's logical that we should like sounds that are pleasing to our ears, soothing to our souls, sounds that are to us intrinsically beautiful. But how about the unpleasant sounds, the strident, screeching, raucous ones?

The shrill whine of an emergency vehicle siren used to well up fear within me and send shudders down my back. I'd shift mental gears long enough to account for the whereabouts and safety of *my* husband, *my* children. Reassured that the emergency could not be on their account, I'd breathe a selfish sigh of relief and go about my selfish business.

Later, we came to understand that even when the sound of tragedy didn't involve *our* immediate family, it did involve someone's child, someone's mother, someone's loved one, and that I shouldn't dismiss it lightly, but should involve myself in intercessory prayer for them. And so the sound of a siren became a call to prayer, but the sound itself still held no beauty for me.

And then one day I heard the siren in the framework of God's love. And it was beautiful. It seemed to say, "Someone's hurt. Everyone, please move out of the way so

---

*Reprinted, with permission, from *The Upper Room Disciplines 1975,* © 1974 by The Upper Room, Nashville, Tennessee.

Thank You, God, that You make everything beautiful in its time. Forgive me that I haven't known the time is now. In Jesus' name. Amen.

For every creature of God is good, and nothing to be refused, if it be received with thanksgiving.

I Timothy 4:4

The Eye of the Beholder*

"Lord, I do fear / Thou'st made the world too beautiful this year." The lines are from Edna St. Vincent Millay's "God's World." They echo the feelings inside me when I see an indescribable sunset, a hillside of blazing autumn foliage, a fresh-from-our-garden bouquet of double gloriosa daisies. But sunsets are not always spectacular. The brilliant leaves fall and crumble, the daisies wind up on the compost heap.

A few days ago we had a torrential rain about sunset. At dusk, after five members of our family had left for movies and meetings and I had tucked the two little girls in bed for the night, I stepped out the back door to drink in the ethereal glowing quality of the light of the new-washed world. Sitting on the back steps, I looked and listened, my very pores soaking up the wonder of God's creation.

As I sat caught up in the beautiful, I became aware of a dark shape moving in the grass alongside the steps. Once I might have thought, "Ugh—a frog," and returned my gaze to the trees and sky. But now I yearned for a closer look at one of God's creatures I had considered ugly, and so I reached down and gently cupped the lively acrobat in my hands and took him into the house.

The tiny tree frog sat oh-so-still for my magnifying-glass inspection of him in the kitchen sink, almost as if he understood his role in glorifying God. I marveled at his delicate toes, the perfect symmetry of his markings, the soft, white throat that could puff so full of song. From now on, I'd say, "A frog—how beautiful!"

---

*Reprinted, with permission, from *The Upper Room Disciplines 1975* © 1974 by The Upper Room, Nashville, Tennessee.

O Lord, honesty is so beautiful. Pretense is so abominable. Help me learn from my child. In Jesus' name. Amen.

For nothing is secret, that shall not be made manifest.
Luke 8:17

Maria's Prayer*

We were planning a holiday weekend in the mountains where my husband was to attend a judges' conference. One of our teenage daughters wanted to go along; and we were also planning to take Maria, our five-year-old adopted miracle. The night before we were to leave home, I was helping Maria say her bedtime prayers. I thanked God for the good day we'd had and for all the fun we would have together in the mountains. Then I said amen and got up from my knees. Apparently trying to keep me from hearing, Maria added a P.S. prayer in a sincere whisper, "Jesus, I don't want to go."

If beauty is truth and truth beauty, Maria's P.S. prayer was a truly beautiful one. She *didn't* want to go. She'd been announcing that vociferously all day. She was sometimes car-sick, and she was afraid she might miss something on the playground. Besides these drawbacks, there was another that crowned them all: Maria was in the midst of an extremely negative period in her life when anything we suggested automatically met with her intense and vocal disapproval.

Well, Jesus answered her prayer. No, He didn't change our plans and let her stay at home. She hadn't asked Him to do that. She'd just told Him the truth and trusted Him who is the truth to handle the situation. He changed her and gave her a wonderful time.

I've thought many times about Maria's beautiful prayer and about my ugly one—thanking God for a good day when it had been positively wretched, thanking Him for anticipated joy when Maria's negativeness had my every cell cringing at the thought of any togetherness.

---

*Reprinted, with permission, from *The Upper Room Disciplines 1975*, © 1974 by The Upper Room, Nashville, Tennessee.

Thank You, thank You, thank You, Lord. Amen.

What is man, that thou art mindful of him? and the son of man, that thou visitest him? For thou hast made him a little lower than the angels, and hast crowned him with glory and honour.

Psalm 8:4-5

He hath no form nor comeliness, and when we shall see him, there is no beauty that we should desire him. He is despised and rejected of men . . . and we esteemed him not.

Isaiah 53:2-3

The Weeds Need Us*

What are we here for? How can there ever be anything beautiful about us? The psalmist is overpowered with a sense of man's littleness as he contemplates the God who made the moon and stars. Sometimes we wonder why God bothered with human beings. A comic strip character suggested that man was here because "the weeds need the carbon dioxide." There are days when we feel about that purposeful—that if God hadn't made us, the world would have been better off.

Much of this pessimism comes from our failure to be obedient to God. Many other things have gone wrong because we have had a hand in running things. Pollution, war, crime, corruption, auto accidents reflect our human messes.

One day my husband was contemplating the sinful, sorry state of mankind, thinking if he was so ugly to himself, how indescribably hideous he must appear to the eyes of a holy God. As he sat, wrapped in pessimism, deciding that an appropriate solution might be for us all to bury ourselves in the nearest junk heap, God spoke to his heart. The Holy Spirit gave him a vision of a creature more beautiful than any he had ever imagined. The being literally glowed with beauty, perfection. He understood that the vision was man—not as he looks to himself, but as he looks to God, spotless and without blemish.

How can it be? Has God poor eyesight? Will we improve that much? No; but there is a reason: Jesus has died for us. He presents us to God beautiful, faultless, our sins gone, our diseases healed, ourselves made whole. The sin, the ugliness, the unwholesomeness, where are they? Oh, Jesus took them all upon Himself—because He loved us so much.

---

*Reprinted, with permission, from *The Upper Room Disciplines 1975*, © 1974 by The Upper Room, Nashville, Tennessee.

Lord, thank You that You made us to be Your holy temples, that You dwell in the praises of Your people. Hallelujah! Amen.

Let everything that hath breath praise the Lord. Praise ye the Lord!

Psalm 150:6

A Gray Squirrel*

A few days ago I was standing at the kitchen sink when a gray squirrel climbed up and perched on top of a stump outside the window. He sat poised, motionless, in his crisply fluffed coat and beautifully full tail. After a few moments, he turned, presenting his other profile, and stood motionless as before, doing nothing that I could see other than *being* perfect squirrel. That was enough, but I wondered.

In the psalms *everything* is commanded to praise God: "All thy works shall praise thee!" (145:10, KJV). "Praise ye the Lord" is the call of Psalm 148 to the angels, hosts, sun and moon, stars of light, heavens, waters, dragons, deeps, fire, hail, snow, vapors, wind, mountains, hills, trees, beasts, cattle, creeping things, flying fowl, kings, all people, princes, judges, young men, maidens, old men, children (KJV). The 150th psalm crescendos with, "Let every thing that hath breath praise the Lord" (KJV).

Could it be that the squirrel was so beautiful because he was praising God in the only way he could, by *being* perfect squirrel, exactly how God made him?

I have seen the faces of people caught up in the wonder of praising God. You may have seen them, too, if not in person, in paintings of people—an old man, hands folded, head bowed, giving thanks for a loaf of bread; or in news photos of young "Jesus People" walking up out of baptismal waters, their faces uplifted, joy pouring from their lips. Every person, every creature, is beautiful when he or she is praising God.

---

*Reprinted, with permission, from *The Upper Room Disciplines 1975,* © 1974 by The Upper Room, Nashville, Tennessee.

Lord, open our eyes to the true beauty of Yourself—perfect, eternal, the gift of God supplying every need. Amen.

Thine eyes shall see the king in his beauty.

Isaiah 33:17

Beauty Born of Love*

What is the most beautiful thing in all the world? What is beauty? What are its requirements? From where does it come?

Beauty that is only skin deep becomes unbeautiful to us when we see corruption underneath. Beauty is more than visual—it is also good. Beauty is perfect.

John Keats wrote, "A thing of beauty is a joy forever." A static object called beautiful—a flawless precious stone—is a hollow mockery when we are hungry and cannot buy bread. Beauty is eternal joy.

Aristotle called beauty "the gift of God"—nothing man can manufacture for himself. The Epistle of James tells us that every good and perfect gift is from above (1:17).

Plato suggested that a thing *needful* would be beautiful to us—rain on parched earth. Does beauty then depend on our need at a particular time? If so, we could never agree, even within our own self, what was most beautiful to us forever.

Look at one description of Jesus from Isaiah: "In our eyes there was no attractiveness at all, nothing to make us want him. . . . We turned our backs on him and looked the other way when he went by" (53:2-3 TLB). Beauty will not look beautiful to us when our hearts are not right.

Francis of Assisi used to turn his back and look the other way when he threw an alms to a leper. But one day he dismounted from his horse, pressed a coin into a leper's hand, embraced and kissed him. As he did, the leper's face was transfigured before him into the very face of Christ, the Morning Star.

---

*Reprinted, with permission, from *The Upper Room Disciplines 1975,* © 1974 by The Upper Room, Nashville, Tennessee.

At the Beach

I so love vacationing at the ocean, soaking up the marvel of what God has given me to enjoy in His incomprehensible creation. How much He teaches me through it!

I have seen His all-encompassing forgiveness in a little plant that grows on the dunes along the shore:

Compass

Offshore breezes blow
gold-brown beach grass
tracing dry circles
in hot sand

The circles the plant draws, as its leaves are blown by the wind, are a reminder to me of the day when "Jesus bent down and wrote with his finger on the ground" (John 8:6 NEB). When He had finished, the woman's accusers were gone, and He said, "Neither do I condemn thee" (John 8:11).

I'd like to be that forgiving.

I have seen God's peace that passes understanding in the

heavy-headed sea oats standing erect in the dead calm on shore while just below them waves are crashing unceasingly.

I've looked at them and marveled that there could be such stability, such peace and calm, in the midst of unending clamor.

That's how I long to be. Full of peace and tranquillity—the peace He gives—not "losing my cool" no matter what goes on about me.

One day I looked out of our rented beach cottage and saw the rainbows of God's promise everywhere along the beach—a whole host of Portuguese men-of-war washed up onto the sand. Their glowing iridescence spoke of God's promise to Noah that He would never again destroy the earth with a flood (Gen. 9:11-17). Oh that everyone could depend on my promises as I can depend on His!

I have caught a glimpse of God's beauty in what I've seen and felt of

Soft lavendar waves
lapping suede sand
at sunset—
a breeze shivering

I've thought of His power in the unceasing surge of tide and waves, and I've been so blessed by it all.

I have seen His love:

The copper-penny moon
shining a golden path
across the ocean
straight to me
no matter where I walk
along the shore

Like God's love
reaching out
across everything
The Light of the world.

Lord, there's so much I don't understand—and so much I do understand. Thank You for opening my eyes—and my heart—so much already, for revealing to me so much of Your peace, Your beauty, Your forgiveness, Your promises, and Your power, Your love. Lord, continually enlarge my heart, that I might hold more of You. In Jesus' name.

The heavens declare the glory of God, and the firmament sheweth his handiwork. Day unto day uttereth speech, and night unto night sheweth knowledge. There is no speech nor language where their voice is not heard.

Psalm 19:1-3

That which is known about God is evident . . . for God made it evident. . . . Since the creation of the world His eternal attributes, His eternal power and divine nature, have been clearly seen, being understood through what has been made. . . .

Romans 1:19-20 NASB

Ask the beasts, and let them teach you;
And the birds of the heavens, and let them
tell you.
Or speak to the earth, and let it teach
you;
And let the fish of the sea declare to you.
Who among all these does not know
That the hand of the Lord has done this
In Whose hand is the life of every
living thing
And the breath of all mankind.

Job 12:7-10 NASB